21st Century
Junior Library

INFOGRAPHICS:
SUPPLY AND DEMAND

Christina Hill

Econo-Graphics Jr.

Published in the United States of America by

CHERRY LAKE PUBLISHING GROUP
Ann Arbor, Michigan
www.cherrylakepublishing.com

Reading Adviser: Beth Walker Gambro, MS, Ed., Reading Consultant, Yorkville, IL

Photo Credits: Cover: grivina/Getty Images; Page 1: ©grivina/Getty Images; Page 9: ©b0red/Pixabay; Page 10: ©Westend61/Getty Images; Page 14: ©SquishyDoom/Getty Images; Page 18: ©Lesia_G/Getty Images, Page 18: ©OpenClipart-Vectors/Pixabay, Page 18: ©teawetyskova/Pixabay; Page 19: ©Youst/Getty Images; Page 19: ©Youst/Getty Images; Page 20: ©digital designer/Pixabay; Page 21: MicrovOne/Getty Images

Cherry Lake Press is an imprint of Cherry Lake Publishing Group.

Library of Congress Cataloging-in-Publication Data
Names: Hill, Christina, author.
Title: Infographics. Supply and demand / Christina Hill.
Other titles: Supply and demand
Description: Ann Arbor, Michigan : Cherry Lake Publishing, [2023] | Series: Econo-graphics Jr. | Includes bibliographical references and index. | Audience: Grades 2-3 | Summary: "Why is it important to understand supply and demand? In the Econo-Graphics Jr. series, young readers will examine economy-related issues from many angles, all portrayed through visual elements. Income, budgeting, investing, supply and demand, global markets, inflation, and more are covered. Each book highlights pandemic-era impacts as well. Created with developing readers in mind, charts, graphs, maps, and infographics provide key content in an engaging and accessible way. Books include an activity, glossary, index, suggested reading and websites, and a bibliography"— Provided by publisher.
Identifiers: LCCN 2022037941 | ISBN 9781668919224 (hardcover) | ISBN 9781668920244 (paperback) | ISBN 9781668921579 (ebook) | ISBN 9781668922903 (pdf)
Subjects: LCSH: Supply and demand—Juvenile literature.
Classification: LCC HB801 .H5225 2023 | DDC 331.12—dc23/eng/20220912
LC record available at https://lccn.loc.gov/2022037941
Cherry Lake Publishing Group would like to acknowledge the work of the Partnership for 21st Century Learning, a network of Battelle for Kids. Please visit http://www.battelleforkids.org/networks/p21 for more information.

Printed in the United States of America
Corporate Graphics

Before embracing a career as an author, **Christina Hill** received a bachelor's degree in English from the University of California, Irvine, and a graduate degree in literature from California State University, Long Beach. When she is not writing about various subjects from sports to economics, Christina can be found hiking, mastering yoga handstands, or curled up with a classic novel. Christina lives in sunny Southern California with her husband, two sons, and beloved dog, Pepper Riley.

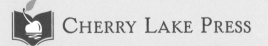

CONTENTS

What Is Supply and Demand?   4

The Laws of Supply and Demand 6

Choices, Competition, and Prices 11

Surplus, Shortage, and Balance   17

Activity   22
Learn More   23
Glossary   24
Index   24

WHAT IS SUPPLY AND DEMAND?

Consumers are people who buy goods and services. Goods are items you can hold in your hands. They include food, clothing, or video games. Services are acts. These include getting your hair cut or attending a sporting event.

All goods and services are affected by **supply** and **demand**. Supply is the amount of goods or services for sale. Demand is the number of consumers willing to pay for the goods or services.

Changing Supply and Demand

If price increases:

Supply

Demand

If price decreases:

Supply

Demand

THE LAWS OF SUPPLY AND DEMAND

The law of demand says that as the price of something goes up, the demand will go down. But if the price of something goes down, the demand for it will go up. Consumers like lower prices because they want to save money.

The law of supply is the opposite of the law of demand.
If the price goes up, the supply will also go up.
If the price goes down, the supply will go down.

Supply and Demand Relationships

DEMAND
- Consumer taste and fads
- Consumer has more spending money
- Prices of related products
- Number of buyers

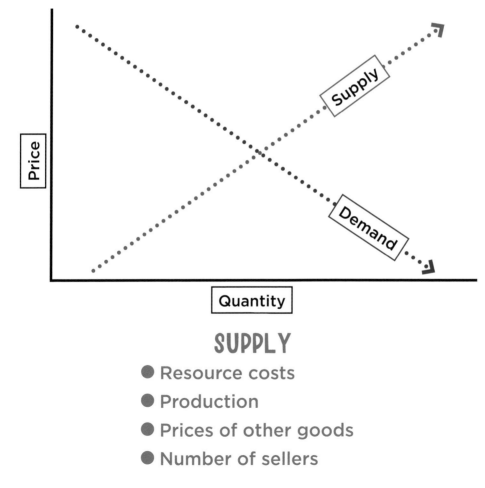

SUPPLY
- Resource costs
- Production
- Prices of other goods
- Number of sellers

Interest in the Term "Fidget Spinner" (2017–2020)

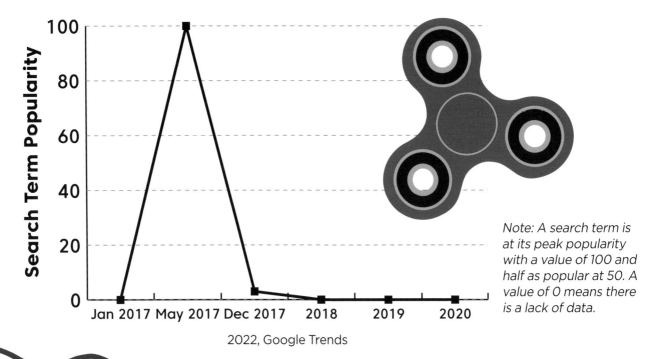

Note: A search term is at its peak popularity with a value of 100 and half as popular at 50. A value of 0 means there is a lack of data.

2022, Google Trends

Fast Facts

- Increased consumer interest sparks demand.
- In 2017, fidget spinners were one of the top-selling toys. This was because of consumer demand.
- Consumers bought 19 million fidget spinners in the first half of 2017.

Stores could not keep up with consumer demand for household goods during the COVID-19 pandemic.

CHOICES, COMPETITION, AND PRICES

Consumers are important in supply and demand. There is competition between producers who offer the same goods or services. Producers can get customers through **advertising**. Other ways are by lowering prices or having sales.

How Location Affects Demand

Starbucks was founded in Washington and remains a West Coast favorite.

Consumers are loyal to brands based on location. Caribou Coffee is the most popular coffee chain in Minnesota. This is where the company was founded.

Dunkin' started in Massachusetts and remains an East Coast favorite.

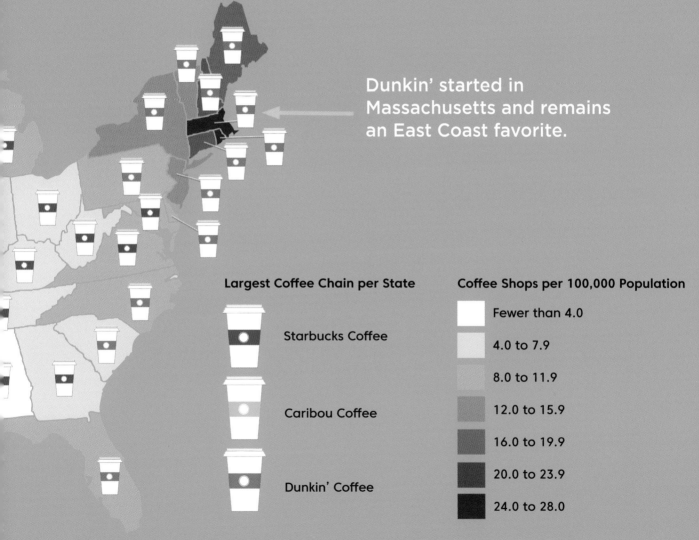

Largest Coffee Chain per State

Starbucks Coffee

Caribou Coffee

Dunkin' Coffee

Coffee Shops per 100,000 Population

Fewer than 4.0

4.0 to 7.9

8.0 to 11.9

12.0 to 15.9

16.0 to 19.9

20.0 to 23.9

24.0 to 28.0

The Demand for Toys

The average American child receives $6,500 worth of toys in their lifetime.

Fast Facts

- In 2018, toy sales were down 1%. Toys "R" Us went out of business.
- In 2019, toy sales were down 3%.
- During the COVID-19 pandemic in 2020, children stayed at home. The demand for toys went way up.

2021, NPD Group; 2021, The Toy Industry Association

COVID-19 Pandemic Toy Sales Surge (2020)

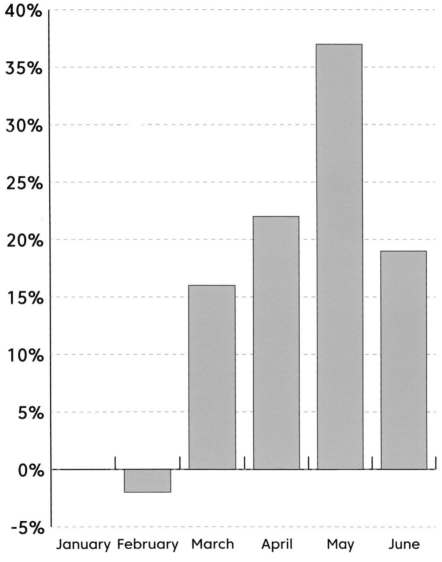

2020, NPD Group

What Is a Free Market?

In a free market, producers sell whatever they want. Consumers can buy whatever they want. There is no law on what the prices will be. There isn't a law on how much of each item producers can sell. The United States is a free market.

PROS

Free markets promote new ideas and new business.

Consumers have more choice.

Free markets promote competition.

CONS

Only successful businesses will remain.

Larger companies are the most powerful.

SURPLUS, SHORTAGE, AND BALANCE

How do producers decide what to charge for their goods and services? The goal in supply and demand is to find a balance. The goal is for supply and demand to be equal.

A **surplus** occurs when the supply is more than the demand. A **shortage** occurs when the demand is more than the supply.

Market Balance for Oranges

At $4 per pound, 800 oranges are supplied.

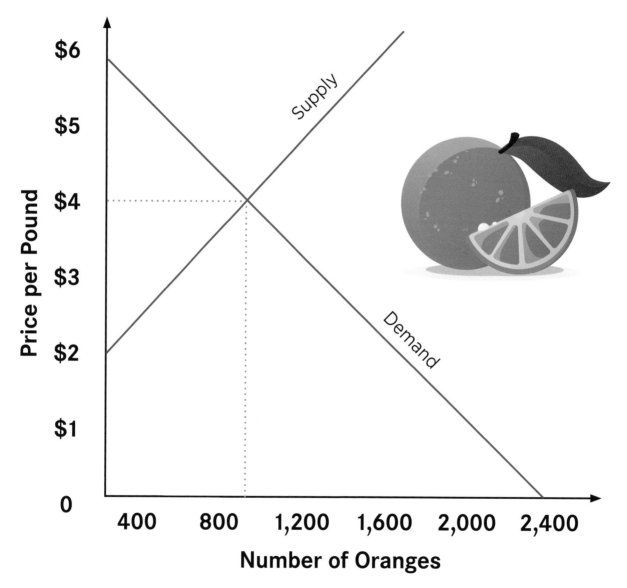

Price per Pound

$6
$5
$4
$3
$2
$1
0

Supply

Demand

400   800   1,200   1,600   2,000   2,400

Number of Oranges

Fast Facts

- Sometimes, a surplus is not a good thing. In 2020, the COVID-19 pandemic caused many schools and restaurants to shut down.

- Dairy farmers were still making the same amount of milk. But the demand for milk dropped by 15% because of the closures.

- Dairy farmers had a surplus of milk but no way to sell it. Prices fell by more than 30% in just 1 month.

2020, NBC News

The Great Toilet Paper Shortage of 2020

In 2020, the COVID-19 pandemic caused people to buy more toilet paper than ever. U.S. stores were left with empty shelves. There was not enough supply to meet the sudden increased demand.

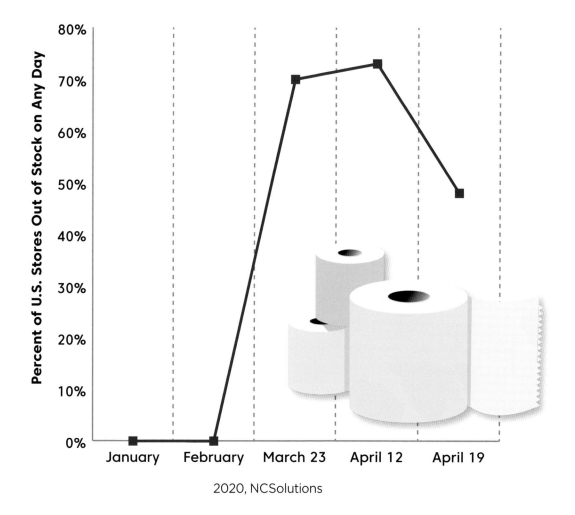

Percent of U.S. Stores Out of Stock on Any Day

| January | February | March 23 | April 12 | April 19 |

2020, NCSolutions

The Goal of Supply and Demand

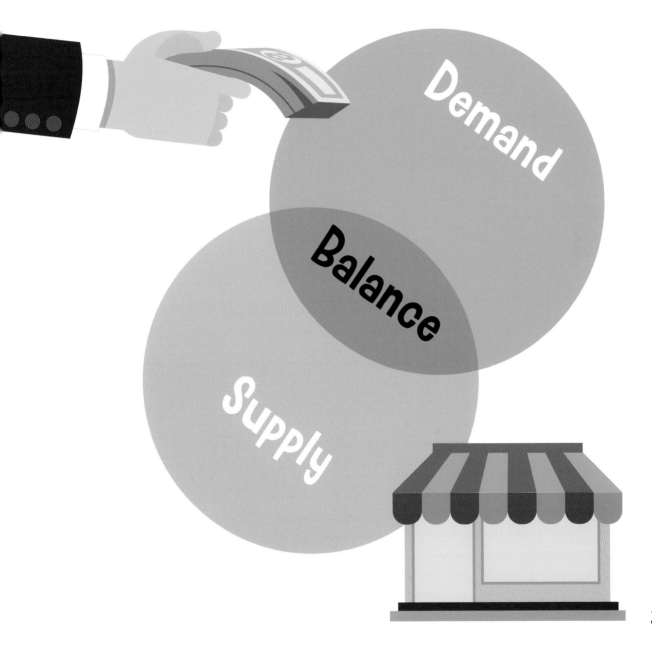

ACTIVITY
Create a Supply and Demand Graph

You notice kids at your school are playing with slime. The demand for slime is growing. You and your best friend find out how to make your own slime. Then you decide to sell it!

Plot the supply curve:

Price	Quantity
$1	1
$2	2
$4	4
$6	6

Plot the demand curve:

Price	Quantity
$1	6
$2	4
$4	2
$6	1

1. What is the balance point of slime price and amount of slime? (Hint: This is the point where the supply and demand lines meet.)

2. What if the glitter you use in the slime increases by $2 per slime container? What will happen to the supply? Explain your answer.

3. What if a famous YouTube star starts advertising that slime is the greatest thing ever? What do you think will happen to the demand? Explain your answer.

LEARN MORE

Books

Lüsted, Marcia Amidon. *Supply and Demand*. New York: Britannica Educational Publishing, 2018.

Ventura, Marne. *Supply and Demand*. Minneapolis, MN: Cody Koala, an imprint of Pop!, 2019.

Websites

Britannica Kids: Supply and Demand
www.britannica.com/topic/supply-and-demand

Investopedia: Law of Supply and Demand
www.investopedia.com/terms/l/law-of-supply-demand.asp

Bibliography

McCluskey, Megan. "*Game On?*" October 20, 2021. https://www.timeforkids.com/g34/game-on-2/?rl=en-910

NFK Editors. "*UK Fuel Supply Problem Causes 'Petrol Panic.'*" September 29, 2021. https://newsforkids.net/articles/2021/09/29/uk-fuel-supply-problem-causes-petrol-panic

NFK Editors. "*US Stores, Banks Deal with Coin Shortage*." August 14, 2020. https://newsforkids.net/articles/2020/08/14/us-stores-banks-deal-with-coin-shortage

GLOSSARY

advertising (AD-vuhr-ty-zing) business of producing materials to help sell a product or service
consumers (kuhn-SOO-muhrz) people who buy goods and services
demand (dih-MAND) desire to purchase goods and services

shortage (SHOR-tij) when there is not enough of something that is needed
supply (suh-PLY) amount of something available to be used
surplus (SUHR-pluhs) amount that is more than the amount needed

INDEX

coffee chains, 12–13
competition, 8, 11, 16
consumers, 4, 16
  demand effects, 8, 9, 10, 11, 14–15, 20
  habits, 6
  location and brand loyalty, 12–13
COVID-19 pandemic, 10, 14, 15, 19, 20

free markets, 16

location, 12–13

market balance, 17, 18, 21

prices
  competition, 8, 11, 16
  supply and demand and, 5, 6–8, 17, 18, 22
production factors, 8, 16, 19

shortages, 10, 17, 20
supply and demand, 4, 6
  activities, 22
  balance, 17, 18, 21
  competition, 8, 11, 16
  global conditions and, 10, 14–15, 19, 20
  laws and relationships, 5, 6–8, 18
  location and, 12–13
surpluses, 17, 19

toilet paper, 20
toys, 9, 14–15, 22